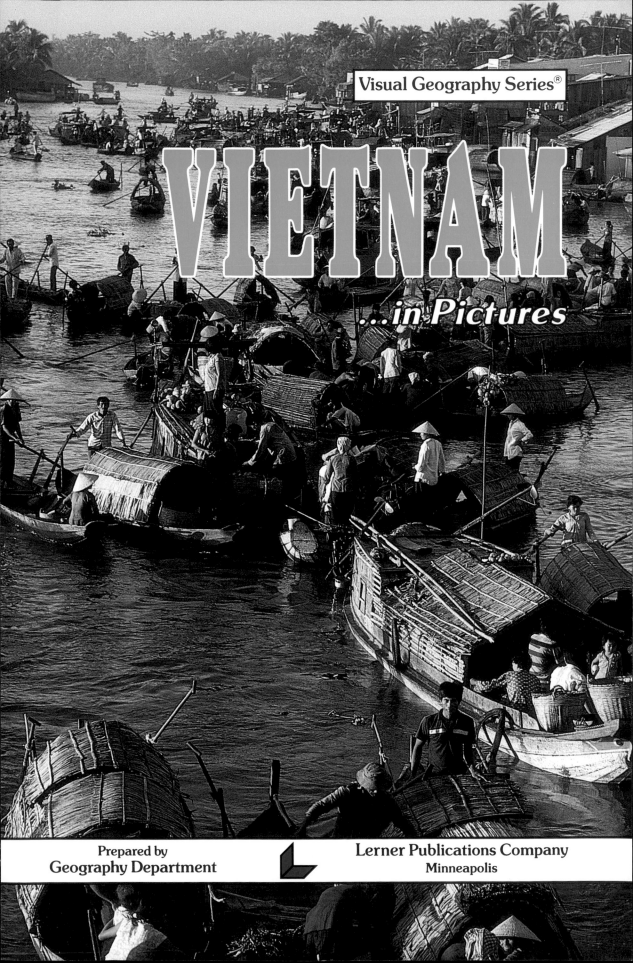

Visual Geography Series®

VIETNAM

...in Pictures

Prepared by
Geography Department

Lerner Publications Company
Minneapolis

Courtesy of Linda James

Using a blunt knife, a Vietnamese girl chops up a large tuber that will be made into animal feed.

This book is a newly commissioned title in the Visual Geography Series. The text is set in 10/12 Century Textbook.

Website address: www.lernerbooks.com

LIBRARY OF CONGRESS CATALOGING-IN-PUBLICATION DATA

Vietnam in pictures. / prepared by Geography Dept., Lerner Publications Co.

  p. cm. — (Visual geography series)
  Includes index.
  ISBN 0–8225–1909–7 (lib. bdg.)
  1. Vietnam—Juvenile literature. [l. Vietnam.]
I. Lerner Publications Company. Geography Dept.
II. Series: Visual geography series (Minneapolis, Minn.)
DS556.3.V48   1994
915.97–dc20   93–21343

International Standard Book Number: 0–8225–1909–7
Library of Congress Catalog Card Number: 93–21343

VISUAL GEOGRAPHY SERIES®

Publisher
Harry Jonas Lerner
Senior Editor
Mary M. Rodgers
Editors
Gretchen Bratvold
Tom Streissguth
Colleen Sexton
Photo Researcher
Erica Ackerberg
Editorial/Photo Assistant
Marybeth Campbell
Consultants/Contributors
Douglas Pike
Sandra K. Davis
Phyllis Schuster
Designer
Jim Simondet
Cartographer
Carol F. Barrett
Indexer
Sylvia Timian
Production Manager
Gary J. Hansen

Courtesy of Linda James

A sculpture of a fierce animal stands under a canopy in Hue, a city in central Vietnam that was once the country's capital.

Acknowledgments

Title page photo © Nevada Wier.

Elevation contours adapted from *The Times Atlas of the World,* seventh comprehensive edition (New York: Times Books, 1985).

2 3 4 5 6 – I/JR – 02 01 00 99 98

Courtesy of Peyton Johnson/FAO

In one of northern Vietnam's many rivers, a woman rows a small, flat-bottomed fishing boat, called a sampan, while her partner casts the net.

Contents

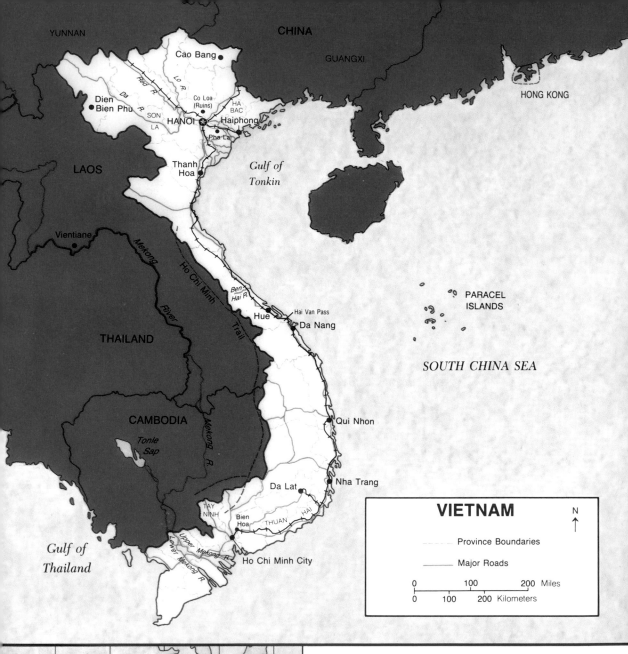

VIETNAM N ↑

Province Boundaries
Major Roads

0   100   200 Miles
0 100 200 Kilometers

VIETNAM
SOUTHEAST ASIA

0   500 Miles
0 500 Kilometers

METRIC CONVERSION CHART
To Find Approximate Equivalents

WHEN YOU KNOW:	MULTIPLY BY:	TO FIND:
AREA		
acres	0.41	hectares
square miles	2.59	square kilometers
CAPACITY		
gallons	3.79	liters
LENGTH		
feet	30.48	centimeters
yards	0.91	meters
miles	1.61	kilometers
MASS		
pounds	0.45	kilograms
tons	0.91	metric tons
VOLUME		
cubic yards	0.77	cubic meters
TEMPERATURE		
degrees Fahrenheit	0.56 (*after* subtracting 32)	degrees Celsius

趙嫗逐吳軍

The Vietnamese leader Trieu Au gathered an army to counter a Chinese invasion in A.D. 248. A popular figure in Vietnamese stories, she is often shown with a sword in either hand while riding on an armored elephant.

Introduction

Located in Southeast Asia, Vietnam is a largely rural nation of nearly 72 million people. The country's first inhabitants settled the Red River Delta 4,000 years ago. The delta (a flat piece of land at the mouth of the river) provided fertile soil in which farmers grew rice and other crops. The settlers eventually set up a kingdom that covered what is now northeastern Vietnam.

China seized the Vietnamese kingdom in 111 B.C. and ruled it for a thousand years. During that time, Chinese culture influenced the Vietnamese, but the conquered people retained their own language and culture and fought for self-rule in frequent rebellions.

The Vietnamese kingdom gained its independence in the tenth century A.D. The country expanded southward, and by the mid-1700s it stretched from the Red River Delta in the north to the Mekong River Delta in the south. At the same time,

5

the fertile land along the South China Sea was attracting European merchants and traders. In the mid-1800s, the French established separate colonies in southern, central, and northern Vietnam.

Southeast Asia, including Vietnam, came under Japanese domination during World War II (1939–1945). After Japan's defeat, the Viet Minh, a group of nationalist and Communist organizations in favor of self-rule, proclaimed Vietnam's independence. France refused to give up its colonies, and war broke out. The Viet Minh's skilled guerrilla fighters defeated the French in 1954. A postwar peace conference split the nation into two parts—North Vietnam and South Vietnam.

North Vietnam adopted Communism, an economic system in which the state owns and controls all farms, banks, and factories. South Vietnam, on the other hand, allowed private ownership of property and supported a free-market system. In South Vietnam, supply and demand—not state controls—determined economic success or failure.

In the 1960s, these differences led to a civil war that drew in several powerful foreign countries. Communist nations, such as the Soviet Union, backed North Vietnam. The United States and other free-market countries supported South Vietnam. Despite the presence of thousands of U.S. troops, North Vietnam gradually gained the upper hand with the use of guerrilla tactics. By 1975 U.S. soldiers had left South Vietnam, which soon fell to the forces of North Vietnam. The two parts of the country were reunited under Communist rule in 1976.

In 1968, when Vietnam's civil war was at its height, a young Vietnamese woman picked through the rubble of her home after a bombing raid.

In recent years, foreign companies have signed contracts with the Vietnamese government to drill offshore for oil in Vietnam's section of the South China Sea.

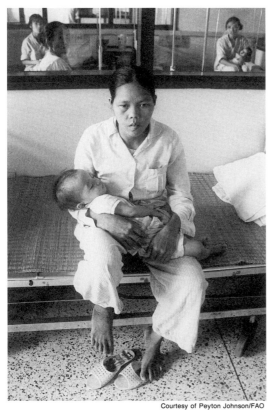

A woman and her child, both suffering from malnutrition, await treatment in a clinic in Hanoi, the Vietnamese capital city.

The reunification of Vietnam caused rejoicing as well as deep concern in the country. The United States ended diplomatic relations with Vietnam and imposed a ban on trade. Badly damaged from the war, the country needed immediate investment to rebuild its farms, factories, power lines, and roads. Most of the aid came from the Soviet Union and other Communist countries. To increase production and to bring the nation under one economic system, the Vietnamese government took over southern farms and businesses. It also set up programs to address the nation's economic problems.

By the late 1980s, however, it was clear that the government's plans were not working. Unemployment was rising, and goods were still in short supply. New leaders saw the need for change and adopted *doi moi,* a package of economic reforms. By the early 1990s, Vietnam's economy was showing signs of recovery and growth. In major cities, small businesses have sprung up, and foreign corporations have opened offices. If progress continues, Vietnam may succeed in providing its people with a better life and a brighter future.

7

The rock formations lining Ha Long Bay, near Hanoi, dwarf boats that frequent the fishing grounds of the South China Sea.

1) The Land

Vietnam stretches along the eastern edge of the Indochinese Peninsula in Southeast Asia. The country, which is shaped like a long capital letter S, covers 127,300 square miles, an area equal to the size of New Mexico.

Vietnam's eastern and southern coasts meet the South China Sea. The Gulf of Tonkin lies off northeastern Vietnam. The southern tip of the country juts into the Gulf of Thailand, another arm of the South China Sea. China is Vietnam's northern neighbor. To the west are Cambodia and Laos.

In addition to its territory on the Asian continent, Vietnam claims ownership of several islands in the South China Sea, including the Paracels and Spratlys. These island groups, which China and the Philippines also claim, occupy areas of ocean that might hold large and valuable reserves of oil.

Topography

Vietnam's varied terrain includes flat, fertile cropland as well as rugged, forested mountains. The Red River and Mekong River deltas together make up 25 percent of the country's area. A long, narrow strip of coastal lowlands connects the two deltas. Hills and mountains, mostly in the north and west, cover the rest of Vietnam.

Except for the lowlands of the Red River Delta, northern Vietnam is mountainous, with some ranges reaching more than 10,000 feet above sea level. About half of these highlands are forested, mostly with evergreens and valuable hardwoods. The country's tallest peak, Fan Si Pan, rises to 10,306 feet near the Chinese border.

The Red River Delta of northern Vietnam has received deposits of waterborne silt for centuries. This fertile soil allows farmers in the region to harvest two, and sometimes three, rice crops each year. The incoming silt also has raised the bed of the Red River, making it shallow at some points. The Vietnamese have built more than 1,800 miles of dikes, canals, and

River-borne silt helps to give the Red River (left) **its distinctive color. At the end of this waterway in northern Vietnam is a delta (a flat area near a river's mouth), where the rich soil nourishes vast fields of rice** (above).

levees to prevent flooding in the region, but surges still cause damage.

Bordering the South China Sea are the sandy coastal lowlands, which in some places narrow to only 30 miles wide. Although not as populated as either delta, the coastal lowlands support fishing and rice farming. Tourism is also important to the region's economy.

West of the coastal lowlands and south of the Red River Delta are the Truong Son Mountains, also called the Annamite Chain. The tallest parts of the range, which stretch westward into Laos, climb to about 8,700 feet above sea level. The Truong Son borders a plateau region in central Vietnam called the Central Highlands. Inhabited by nomadic groups, the Central Highlands have fertile soil that nourishes tea plants and rubber trees.

Larger than the Red River Delta, the Mekong Delta is home to more than half the population of southern Vietnam and is the country's main farming area. The delta's rich soils, deposited by the Mekong and its feeder rivers, are especially suited to rice growing.

Rivers

The 500-mile-long Red River begins in Yunnan province of southern China and marks a 30-mile section of the Vietnamese-Chinese border. The rapidly flowing waterway enters Vietnam northwest of the capital city of Hanoi and is eventually joined by the Lo River and the Da River. The Red River divides into branches that cross the delta and empty into the Gulf of Tonkin at five different locations.

The Mekong River starts its 2,600-mile course in China and forms part of the borders of Myanmar (formerly Burma), Thailand, and Laos. As it enters Cambodia, the Mekong broadens and eventually divides into two main branches—the Lower River and the Upper River. After arriving in Vietnam, the Lower River flows directly into the South China Sea. The Upper River splits into six branches before reaching the sea. These rivers carry enormous amounts of fertile soil from the mountains to the delta lowland.

During the rainy season, the surging Mekong backs up into Tonle Sap, a large lake in Cambodia. This natural reservoir and a system of artificial canals reduce the danger of flooding and prevent the Mekong River Delta from drying out between rainy seasons.

Although the Red and Mekong rivers dominate Vietnam's waterway system, the country has dozens of smaller rivers. Most of these streams rise in the northern or western mountains and flow eastward toward the South China Sea. One of these waterways—the Ben Hai River—once marked the boundary between North and South Vietnam.

Farmers use buckets to bring water to rice crops in the Mekong River Delta of southern Vietnam.

Workers transport a shipment of gravel on the Perfume River, which runs through the city of Hue in central Vietnam.

Climate

Vietnam lies entirely within the tropics, an area of warm temperatures and little seasonal change. Nevertheless, the country's climate varies from south to north because of differences in terrain and altitude.

Temperatures remain steady in the south, where the average reading is 81° F throughout the year. April and May are the hottest and most humid months. In April the average high in Ho Chi Minh City (formerly Saigon) is 95° F, and the average low is 76° F. In December, the south's coldest month, the high is 87° F and the low is 71° F.

The northern provinces have a cool season from December to March. In January, the coldest month, Hanoi's average daily high and low readings are 68° F and 56° F, respectively. In June, the warmest month, high and low readings are 91° F and 78° F.

Monsoons (seasonal, rain-bearing winds) determine Vietnam's patterns of rainfall. From May to October, southwestern monsoons sweep across southern Vietnam, the Central Highlands, and the northern mountains. These winds bring short, daily downpours. Winter monsoons, which arrive from the northeast between November and March, pick up moisture from the South China Sea. As the winds move inland, they dump rainfall on the northern half of Vietnam. Most parts of the country receive nearly 80 inches of annual precipitation, but some sections of the Central Highlands get 130 inches.

11

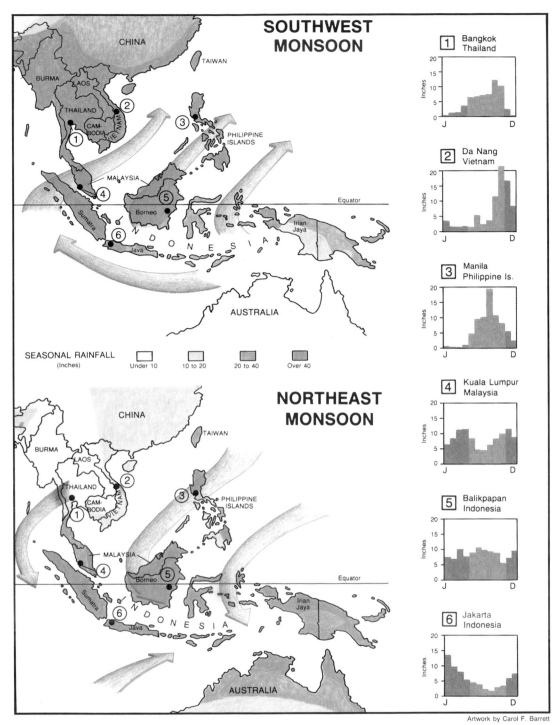

SOUTHWEST MONSOON

1 Bangkok Thailand

2 Da Nang Vietnam

3 Manila Philippine Is.

SEASONAL RAINFALL (Inches) — Under 10 | 10 to 20 | 20 to 40 | Over 40

NORTHEAST MONSOON

4 Kuala Lumpur Malaysia

5 Balikpapan Indonesia

6 Jakarta Indonesia

Artwork by Carol F. Barrett

These maps show the seasonal shift of winds, called monsoons, over Southeast Asia and the rainfall levels for six cities in the region. From May to October, the winds blow from the southwest. From November to April, they come from the northeast. Because the monsoons in Southeast Asia travel over the ocean, they bring rain to coastal and island areas. The southwest monsoon carries rain to Southeast Asia and to islands north of the equator. These areas are dry during the northeast monsoon period. Islands south of the equator receive moisture from the northeast monsoon but are relatively dry during the southwest monsoon period. Both monsoons bring rain to islands along the equator. Da Nang, Vietnam, receives most of its rain from September through November, during the southwest monsoon. (Data taken from *World-Climates* by Willy Rudloff, Stuttgart, 1981.)

In February and March, a persistent drizzle that the Vietnamese nickname "rain dust" falls in the north. Between July and November, violent storms called typhoons sometimes develop over the ocean and hit northern and central Vietnam with destructive force.

Flora and Fauna

Centuries ago, vast tropical forests of teak, mahogany, dipterocarps, and other hard-woods covered the highest elevations of Vietnam. At slightly lower levels, species of pine and other evergreens flourished. Mangrove trees, which local people cut and burned as cooking fuel, grew in swampy coastal regions. Only about one-fourth of these original forests remain.

The deforestation has resulted from increasing demands for farmland and wood by a growing population. Nomadic peoples in the Central Highlands have cleared away trees to create cropland. Many trees

Photo © Doan Thi Nam-Hau

Water lilies *(left)* root in muddy riverbeds and send their flowering stalks upward through the water. A group of Vietnamese from the Central Highlands *(below)* show off a python that is many feet long.

Photo by Rick Graetz, *Montana Magazine*

A farmer tends her flock of ducks, which she raises for food and to sell at open-air markets.

were lost during the Vietnam War of the 1960s and 1970s. To uncover the hideouts of opposing forces, U.S. planes destroyed huge areas of forested land through bombing or chemical spraying.

A national plan to reforest Vietnam began in the mid-1980s. Work crews planted hundreds of millions of trees, mostly non-native eucalyptus and acacia. In the shade of these species, foresters raise seedlings of bamboo, dipterocarps, and other valuable kinds of timber.

Vietnam's warm, wet climate is ideal for the growth of many types of flowers and plants. Lush orchids thrive near the resort city of Da Lat, where florists ship the flowers to worldwide markets. Epiphytes—rootless plants that hang on trees—take their nourishment from particles in the air. The fingerlike shoots of lianas cling to the trunks of tropical trees.

The loss of forested land deprived many animals of their habitats. The Javan rhinoceros and the kouprey (a forest ox), for example, have very limited ranges and are in danger of becoming extinct. Yet Vietnam still contains more than 270 species of mammals, including elephants, tigers, leopards, black bears, serows (mountain goats), and bantengs (wild oxen). New laws that limit hunting help to protect these species, as well as primates, such as langurs, gibbons, and macaques.

Vietnam is home to 180 kinds of reptiles, including crocodiles, pythons, and cobras. Amphibians and fish also thrive in the country's tropical climate. More than 700 bird species live and breed in Vietnam, especially in the deltas and along the coasts. Farmers raise partridges, ducks, and other birds as sources of food.

Natural Resources

Northern Vietnam contains most of the country's natural resources. Large deposits of coal, a major source of fuel, are located near Hanoi. Factories in the port of Haiphong process some of the region's stocks of phosphates, a mineral used in making fertilizer. Other mineral resources include zinc, tin, manganese, and bauxite (the raw material for making aluminum).

Vietnam's dwindling forests still provide hardwoods, particularly mahogany and teak, for the furniture and building industries. Foreign contracts to tap offshore oil reserves in the South China Sea will earn much-needed income. After refining, this oil will also help to meet some of Vietnam's own energy demands.

The waters in and around Vietnam are a source of saltwater and freshwater fish, chiefly shrimp, crab, lobster, mackerel, and tuna. Much of the catch is sold locally, but workers process some for export.

Cities

Twenty percent of Vietnam's 75.1 million people live in urban areas, the largest being Ho Chi Minh City, Hanoi, and Haiphong. Important secondary cities include Da Nang, Hue, and Nha Trang, all of which lie along the coast of central Vietnam.

HO CHI MINH CITY (SAIGON)

Saigon and its surrounding area in the Mekong Delta are home to 3.9 million people. The city's seldom-used official name—Ho Chi Minh City—honors the Communist leader who fought for Vietnam's independence from France.

Founded in the sixth century A.D. by the Khmer of Cambodia, Saigon belonged to the Khmer Empire until the 1600s. At that time, the Vietnamese pushed southward and settled the lands around Saigon, which became a busy port. The port attracted

Courtesy of T. Loftas/FAO

Members of a fishing crew sort through the day's catch from the South China Sea.

Photo © William Short

Market stalls, construction cranes, scooters, and cyclos clog a street in Ho Chi Minh City (formerly Saigon), the main urban area in southern Vietnam.

the French, who made Saigon a colonial capital in the mid-1800s. They constructed broad streets and European-style buildings in the city's neighborhoods, many of which still have a French look.

During the Vietnam War, thousands of U.S. troops, journalists, and civilians filled the hotels, nightclubs, and cafes of Saigon, whose economy was closely tied to wartime activity. After the war ended, the city's economy slowed. Many businesses closed, and others were seized by the government. In recent years, however, economic improvements have caused night spots to reopen, and many new hotels and businesses are under construction. Street vendors now do a brisk business, and bicycles, cyclos (bicycle taxis), and motor scooters crowd the city's avenues.

The financial and commercial center of southern Vietnam, Saigon is slowly recovering from decades of war. The city's

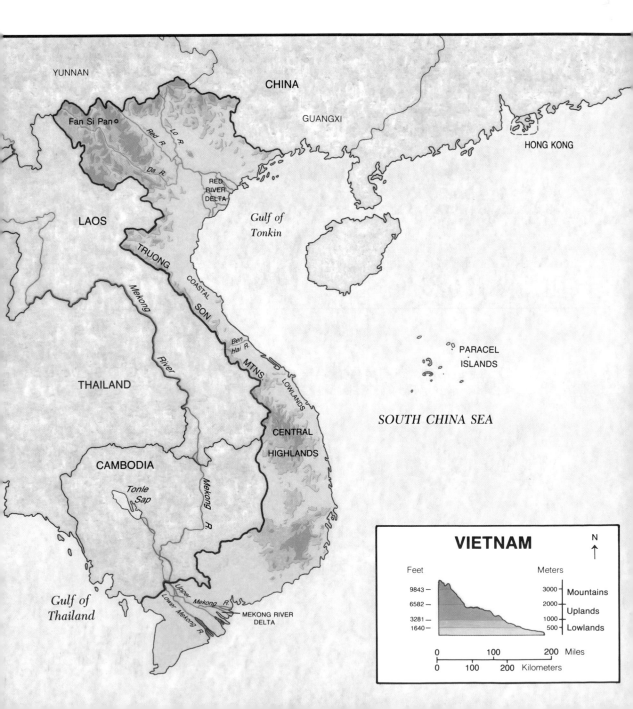

About four million people live and work in crowded Ho Chi Minh City and its surrounding suburbs.

factories process food and make household items, including furniture and carpets. Small, family-owned businesses are flourishing, and outdoor food markets that once lacked goods now display a wide variety of fruits and vegetables.

HANOI

Some 3.1 million people live in the 11 districts that make up Greater Hanoi, Vietnam's second largest urban center. Four of the districts form the capital city of Hanoi (population 925,000), the industrial hub of northern Vietnam. Factories in the city manufacture bicycles, cigarettes, farm equipment, and wood products. Recent economic reforms have encouraged foreign investments in Hanoi, and as a result many private businesses have opened.

Located along the Red River 45 miles inland from the Gulf of Tonkin, Hanoi began as the capital of the Ly dynasty (an early Vietnamese family of rulers) in 1010. The city continued to be an important cultural and educational center after the Vietnamese kingdom moved its capital to Hue in the 1800s.

Traffic is heavy in front of Hanoi's French-built Roman Catholic cathedral, where religious services are still held.

In the heart of downtown Hanoi is Hoan Kiem Lake (Lake of the Restored Sword). In the surrounding park, residents hold festivals, bike races, and dove-flying competitions. South of the lake is a modern commercial section, where French-colonial buildings house hotels and large stores. North of Hoan Kiem Lake is Hanoi's old quarter, the site of ancient temples and of Ho Chi Minh's mausoleum (above-ground tomb).

HAIPHONG

Situated 64 miles east of the capital on the Gulf of Tonkin, Haiphong (population 1.4 million) is the principal seaport of Hanoi and of northern Vietnam. Goods shipped into Haiphong go by rail to the capital. In the harbor, dozens of small boats compete for space with barges, tugboats, and cargo vessels. Plans are under way to update and enlarge the port to accommodate bigger ships.

Established by the French in the late 1800s, Haiphong came under Japanese rule in World War II. During the Vietnam

Photo © Nevada Wier

At a streetside stall in the capital, a seller offers passersby dishes of fish and vegetables flavored with a variety of spices.

Photo by Rick Graetz, *Montana Magazine*

Boats of all sizes throng the harbor at Haiphong, the main port of northern Vietnam.

A sampan glides within sight of the Citadel, a nineteenth-century stronghold at Hue.

War, most of North Vietnam's imported military supplies arrived in Haiphong. As a result, the port became the target of heavy U.S. bombing. Repairs of wartime damage are still being made in some parts of the city.

Haiphong's major industries produce ships, canned fish, glass, and woolen carpets. A few plants process phosphates into farm fertilizers. Generating stations transfer electricity from nearby hydropower stations to Haiphong's factories. In keeping with the city's seafaring past, Haiphong is also the site of two naval schools.

SECONDARY CITIES

Da Nang (population 370,000) sits midway along the country's eastern coast. The city's port facilities, which have been rebuilt since the 1970s, serve central Vietnam and landlocked Laos. During the Vietnam War, Da Nang's huge U.S.-built air base saw the arrival of many service people, who relaxed at the local beaches when on leave. Now the base is quiet, and the resale of military scrap metal is an im-

portant part of the local economy. Marble Mountain, which rises above the city, gives visitors a broad view of Da Nang and its surroundings. Some of the mountain's caves hold important religious shrines.

Hue (population 260,000) is located 45 miles north of Da Nang and 11 miles inland from the coast. Established in 1802 by Emperor Gia Long, Hue was Vietnam's capital until 1945 and remains a cultural, religious, and educational center. The Citadel, a stronghold built by Gia Long, dominates the city from its site along the Perfume River.

Once part of the kingdom of Champa, Nha Trang (population 263,000) is an important fishing port on Vietnam's southeastern coast. A local fleet of more than 10,000 small boats brings in lobster, shrimp, scallops, abalone, mackerel, and other varieties of seafood. The production of salt from nearby deposits employs thousands of the city's workers. Nha Trang also exports cash crops—such as latex from rubber trees and tea from tea plants—that are grown in the surrounding area.

The curving beach at Nha Trang, a city in southeastern Vietnam, welcomes fishing boats as well as sunbathers.

19

Dating to roughly the tenth century A.D., this glazed stoneware container comes from the city of Thanh Hoa, northern Vietnam.

2) History and Government

The history of Vietnam begins in the Red River Delta, where the ancestors of the modern Vietnamese lived at least 4,000 years ago. These people later moved southward in search of more farmland. In what is now central Vietnam, they met the Cham—a people ethnically related to modern Cambodians—and the Khmer, who controlled the Mekong River Delta. Early contacts with the Cham and the Khmer eventually brought conflict. By the mid-1700s A.D., the Vietnamese had defeated their rivals and were occupying all of the land that makes up modern Vietnam.

Early Kingdoms

Excavations of ancient sites indicate that the first large, centrally organized state in the Red River Delta emerged around 800 B.C., a time known as the Dong-son period. The Dong-son people built dikes and canals to control the rivers of the delta. They used the tides of the South China Sea to irrigate their rice fields, which were called *lacs.* By protecting the land from floods and droughts and by irrigating, the Dongson produced dependable harvests.

Using small ships and canoes, the Dongson people also traveled and traded. Through trading contacts on the Indochinese Peninsula, they expanded their knowledge of metalworking and learned to mold bronze into farm tools, weapons, and drums.

By 250 B.C., a Vietnamese ruler named An Duong Vuong had created the Au Lac kingdom by bringing together the Dongson of the delta and peoples of the neighboring highlands. The Au Lac capital, at Co Loa, was 20 miles north of present-day Hanoi. Most of the kingdom's people were rice farmers who worked lacs that belonged to local nobles.

Zhao Tuo, a Chinese commander, conquered the Red River Delta in 207 B.C. and set up Nam Viet, an independent kingdom that recognized the supreme authority of the Chinese emperors. (In Chinese, *Nam* means "south," and *Viet* refers to the peoples living along China's southern frontier.) In 111 B.C., a wave of Chinese imperial armies seized Nam Viet and made it a Chinese province.

The culture of China changed Vietnamese society. The Chinese philosophy of Confucianism, for example, provided Vietnam with a strict system for governing and for daily life. The Vietnamese also adopted the Chinese picture characters that Confucian officials and educators used for reading and writing.

Photo © Nevada Wier

Hundreds of years ago, Vietnamese farmers grew abundant crops of rice, which helped early communities to prosper.

China took over northern Vietnam in the second century B.C. and made it a Chinese province. Among Chinese influences brought to the province were the teachings of Confucius *(right),* **a Chinese official whose philosophy about living and working was spread throughout Asia by his students.**

Photo by Bettmann Archive

Some rich Vietnamese nobles—including two sisters, Trung Trac and Trung Nhi—resisted Chinese ways. The sisters led a rebellion in A.D. 39 that restored Nam Viet's independence. But most of the local aristocracy failed to support the Trung sisters, and China's overwhelming power helped it reassert control in A.D. 42.

Chinese rule of Vietnam lasted a thousand years. During that time, educated Vietnamese accepted some aspects of Chinese culture, including the Chinese form of the Buddhist faith. The Chinese also taught Vietnamese workers to breed silkworms, to mint coins, and to manufacture porcelain. Along Vietnam's coasts, the Chinese constructed several harbors to foster international trade. Some Vietnamese families acquired wealth and power as trade increased.

Independence and Conquest

In the tenth century, political upheavals in China gave the Vietnamese a chance to challenge Chinese rule. Led by Ngo Quyen, a rebel army defeated the Chinese and declared Vietnam's independence in 939. Ngo set up a capital at Co Loa but did not live long enough to create a strong state. After Ngo's death in 944, the region's wealthy landowning families competed for power.

In 1009 Ly Cong Uan, the head of one of these families, seized control and later founded the capital of his Ly dynasty on the site of modern Hanoi. The country—which was renamed Dai Viet (Greater Viet)—developed an effective central government that was organized according to Confucian ideas. Confucian scholars had to train for years and then pass tough civil-service examinations before joining the

Photo from Maurice Durand Collection of Vietnamese Art, Yale University Library

The aristocratic sisters Trung Trac and Trung Nhi spearheaded a rebellion against Chinese rule in A.D. 39. They massed an army of supporters and set up a short-lived kingdom that stretched from southern China to Hue. The Chinese defeated the sisters three years later. Rather than be taken prisoner, Trung Trac and Trung Nhi drowned themselves in a river.

The Vietnamese general Tran Hung Dao *(center)* used guerrilla tactics to defeat the army of the Mongols, who invaded Vietnam from China in 1287. After news arrived that a Mongol fleet of 400 ships was about to attack, Tran Hung Dao ordered metal stakes to be driven into the bed of a river in northern Vietnam. At low tide, a small number of Vietnamese boats lured the larger Mongol fleet into the river. The Vietnamese then attacked the trapped ships, burning the fleet and forcing the Mongols to retreat.

mandarins. This elite group of bureaucrats ran the government.

During the Ly reign, the Vietnamese began to move southward in search of new fields for rice cultivation. In central Vietnam lay the unplanted lands of the Cham. Vietnamese armies attacked the Cham kingdom, called Champa, and forced the Champa ruler to give up some of his provinces. Vietnamese farmers began to cultivate rice in the coastal lowlands, where engineers built dikes and canals to control flooding.

The Ly dynasty lasted until 1225, when the Tran family came to power by having one of its members marry the Ly heiress. Tran rulers further improved the country's administration and economy. Water-control projects allowed farmers to plant more crops and produce bigger harvests, which led to economic prosperity. Mandarins continued to guide the country, and the Buddhist religion flourished.

In the late 1200s, Mongol armies from eastern Asia attacked Dai Viet. General Tran Hung Dao fought back and defeated the invaders. Throughout the 1300s, Tran armies also skirmished with Champa over the provinces it still had in central Vietnam. Seeking help, Champa's ruler asked the Chinese to attack the Vietnamese kingdom. As a result, by 1407 Dai Viet had lost its independence to the Chinese Empire.

The Chinese emperor required local nobles to wear Chinese clothing and banned the teaching of the Vietnamese language.

The ruins of a seventh-century tower from the days of the Champa kingdom stand in central Vietnam near Nha Trang. The Champa realm flourished from the second century to the late fourteenth century. During the 1400s, the Vietnamese armies of Le Thanh Tong conquered it.

China's harsh rule soon stirred revolts in Vietnam. Le Loi, a wealthy landowner, organized a resistance movement that expelled the Chinese in 1427. He set up the Le dynasty, whose capital was in present-day Hanoi.

Under the Le kings, Dai Viet enjoyed political stability and a golden age of Confucian culture. Le Thanh Tong, one of the greatest of the Le rulers, established a new legal system and ordered the writing of a 15-volume history of Dai Viet. He also expanded Vietnam's territory southward by completely annexing (taking over) Champa in the 1470s.

Division and Unity

After Le Thanh Tong's death in 1497, weak Le rulers ignored the well-organized Confucian system of governing, and the central government fell apart. In the early 1500s, strong clans (family groups) fought one another for power. In 1527 Mac Dang Dung, the head of one clan, overthrew the Le rulers, and a long civil war broke out.

By the late sixteenth century, two families dominated the country. The Trinh family, the real power in the north, reinstated the weak Le monarchs to serve as figurehead rulers (rulers in name only). In the south, the Nguyen family exercised control but publicly said it was loyal to the Le government.

At the same time, the Nguyens were using their armies to annex land belonging to the Khmer Empire. The Khmer controlled a broad section of the Indochinese Peninsula, including the fertile Mekong Delta. Determined to gain more territory, the Nguyens sent farmers into Khmer lands. By 1690 Vietnamese people had entered Saigon, a Khmer settlement within the Mekong Delta.

Rain and wind have lashed the temple statues at Angkhor, Cambodia, the capital of the ancient Khmer Empire, which included the Mekong River Delta. Forces from Vietnam's powerful Nguyen family annexed (took over) the delta in the 1600s.

The Nguyen family also increased its international trade links by supplying silks and precious metals to Chinese, Japanese, and European merchants. Farmers on Nguyen plantations grew sugar and other crops for world markets. Meanwhile, European traders, accompanied by Roman Catholic missionaries, worked hard to build trade and to win Vietnamese converts to Christianity.

Despite the expanding power of the Nguyen family, the Vietnamese who settled in the Mekong Delta wanted to be independent of Vietnam's rulers. In 1771 three brothers led a rebellion from Tay Son, a village located in eastern Vietnam. In the 1780s, after several years of fighting, the Tay Son army drove Nguyen forces from the Mekong Delta and then defeated the Trinh army in the north.

After taking over northern, central, and southern Vietnam, the brothers tried to set up a unified government. The Tay Son regime, however, could not solve the problems caused by years of war, such as damaged farms, poor harvests, and famine.

In the late 1700s and early 1800s, the author Nguyen Du worked at the royal courts of the Trinh, the Tay Son, and the Nguyen families. His epic work, *The Tale of Kieu*, details the troubles of a beautiful young Vietnamese woman named Kieu. Villains in the piece include Miss Hoan *(left)*, who is jealous of Kieu's looks, and Dame Tu *(right)*, who wants to make Kieu into a prostitute.

In nearby Thailand, a young survivor of the Nguyen clan, Nguyen Phuc Anh, planned to regain Vietnam. He got the backing of France and other foreign powers, which were setting up commercial outposts in Asia. Nguyen Phuc Anh's forces marched north from the Mekong Delta and finally defeated the Tay Son army in 1802. After his forces overran most of present-day Vietnam, Nguyen Phuc Anh founded the Nguyen imperial dynasty and named himself Emperor Gia Long.

Gia Long built his capital city at Hue in central Vietnam. He strengthened the Confucian bureaucracy and crushed all opposition to his government. During his reign, Gia Long grew increasingly suspicious of French Catholic missionaries. The priests were not only converting many Vietnamese to Christianity but also were meddling in imperial court politics. He restricted the activities of the French in his country and banned Christianity among his subjects.

In the 1830s, Gia Long's son and successor, Minh Mang, shared his father's dislike of French influence. Even after the emperor executed dozens of French missionaries, some continued to work in Vietnam and to call for a French takeover of the region.

French Control

French merchants of the 1840s were eager to exploit Vietnam's economic resources. They pressured the French emperor, Napoleon III, to invade. A French fleet successfully attacked Da Nang in 1858 but was unable to hold onto the port. After the French captured Saigon the next year, they forced the Nguyen ruler to give up the Mekong Delta. By 1867 France had established the region as the French colony of Cochin China.

French troops advanced farther north in the early 1880s, attacking Hue and the Red River Delta. By the end of the decade, central Vietnam (called Annam) and northern Vietnam (called Tonkin) were in French hands. France combined these two regions with Cochin China, Cambodia, and Laos—which France also controlled—to form the Indochinese Union. A French-appointed governor-general oversaw the union, while the Nguyen monarch became the figurehead ruler.

Photo © Richard L. Carlton

The Vietnamese emperor Gia Long built the Citadel in Hue in the early 1800s. Enclosed by huge stone walls, the Citadel resembles a small city. In the center of the complex—a set of buildings called the Forbidden City—lived the emperor and his family.

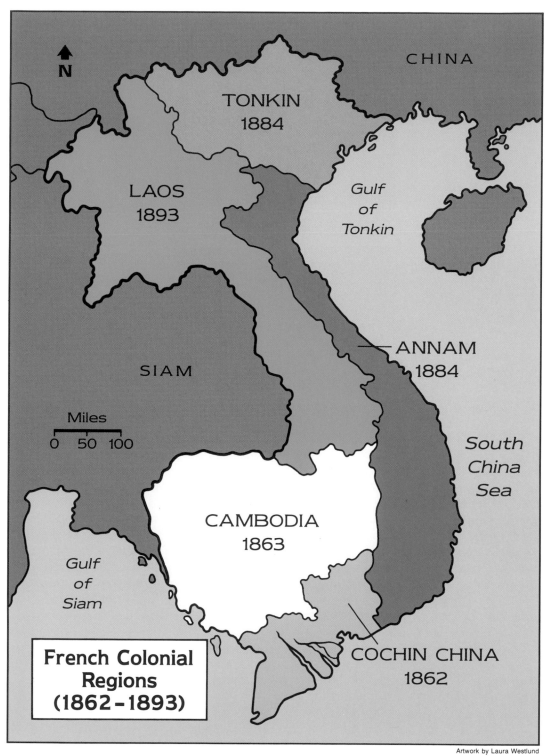

French Colonial Regions (1862–1893)

N

TONKIN
1884

CHINA

LAOS
1893

Gulf
of
Tonkin

ANNAM
1884

SIAM

Miles
0 50 100

South
China
Sea

Gulf
of
Siam

CAMBODIA
1863

COCHIN CHINA
1862

Throughout the 1800s, the French government sought ways to control parts of Southeast Asia, which includes modern Vietnam, Laos, Cambodia, and Thailand (then called Siam). Attacks and treaties eventually allowed the French to establish several colonies. The three French colonial regions in Vietnam were Tonkin, Annam, and Cochin China.

Photo from Maurice Durand Collection of Vietnamese Art, Yale University Library

An artwork from the colonial era shows young Vietnamese attending schools set up and run by French teachers.

Colonial administrators developed and exploited Vietnam's natural resources. To expand rice production in the Mekong Delta, the French drained swamps and built irrigation systems. The colonial government gave land along the Cambodian border to French settlers, who established large farms and rubber plantations. Landowners in the sparsely populated Central Highlands cultivated tea and other cash crops for export. In the north, the French mined coal and minerals.

The French used Vietnamese laborers to build ports, roads, bridges, and railway lines to ship goods to market. The economic development of Vietnam did not benefit the local people, however. Most farmers worked for landowners who did not live on the farms they owned. These absentee landlords exported the crops instead of selling them locally. Having lost their land, many Vietnamese had to find work in coal mines or on rubber plantations, where the pay was low and the working conditions were hard.

RESISTANCE MOVEMENTS AND WORLD WAR II

The harshness of French colonial rule strengthened Vietnamese opposition to the Indochinese Union. Poor farmers protested high taxes, government corruption, and the growing power of absentee landowners. In the early twentieth century, a group of Vietnamese scholars set up an association that sought to overthrow French rule and to establish a constitutional government.

In the 1920s, the Communist philosophy of Vladimir Lenin, the leader of the Soviet Union, inspired a new generation of nationalists, including a young activist named Ho Chi Minh. Communists favored the state ownership of all property, including farms, factories, and mines. During a stay in France, Ho became active in the French Communist party, which encouraged him to organize a Communist movement in his homeland. By 1930 Ho had formed the Indochinese Communist party (ICP).

During the worldwide economic depression of the 1930s, the Vietnamese struggled to survive, and political unrest largely ceased. The ICP used this peaceful time to broaden its support among farmers, factory workers, and managers. The party was especially successful in Annam and Tonkin, where the depression was causing much anti-French feeling. By the end of the 1930s, a number of nationalist, non-

Communist parties also existed in Vietnam. They and the ICP strongly opposed French colonial power.

Meanwhile, the strong Japanese Empire to the northeast of Vietnam was threatening Southeast Asia. By 1942 Japan was fighting Britain and the United States in World War II and had taken over the entire Indochinese Peninsula. In exchange for the right to use Vietnam's military facilities and to station troops in Vietnam, the Japanese allowed the French to remain in charge of the Indochinese Union.

The leaders of many nationalist parties, including the ICP, retreated to southern China, where they formed a united front to oppose Japan and to win Vietnam's independence. This organization—called the Viet Minh, or Vietnam Independence League—prepared its members to stage a postwar revolt against the French.

The First Indochina War

On August 7, 1945, Japan surrendered to Britain and the United States, and World War II ended. Within days the Viet Minh set up a temporary government in Hanoi headed by Ho Chi Minh, who formed the independent Democratic Republic of Vietnam (DRV). Although strong in Tonkin and Annam, the Viet Minh did not have as much support in Cochin China. French officials in the south and the DRV could not agree on how to govern Vietnam. Tensions grew, and in December 1946 war broke out.

For the next eight years, fighting raged between the Viet Minh and the French—a conflict the Vietnamese call the First Indochina War. The French used superior weapons to seize strategic airfields and cities. The Viet Minh, on the other hand, trained its guerrilla troops to attack French outposts in the countryside. In May 1954, the Viet Minh defeated the French at Dien Bien Phu, a town in northwestern Vietnam. As a result, France decided to settle for peace. At a conference

Born in 1890 in central Vietnam, Ho Chi Minh was an early champion of the political philosophy of Communism and later founded the Indochinese Communist party. During World War II (1939–1945), Ho gathered an army, called the Viet Minh, and planned a postwar rebellion to gain Vietnam's independence from France.

in Geneva, Switzerland, France agreed to the independence of its Indochinese colonies.

The conference divided Vietnam into two zones, whose dividing line would be along the Ben Hai River. North Vietnam, or the DRV, remained under the control of the Communists, who were led by the party's general secretary, Ho Chi Minh. Bao Dai, the last Nguyen monarch, became head of the government of the Associated State of Vietnam, also called South Vietnam.

The peace agreement instructed both governments to cease hostilities and to prepare for national elections that would reunify Vietnam. Although Bao Dai supported the cease-fire, he did not back the elections. DRV officials, who thought the southern government was weak and would quickly fall, supported national elections to begin reunification.

Two Vietnams

Bao Dai's prime minister, Ngo Dinh Diem, used harsh measures to stabilize the South Vietnamese government. Diem's growing power made him a strong rival for the country's leadership. In October 1955, he defeated Bao Dai in a public vote in the south and proclaimed himself president of the newly named Republic of Vietnam.

Popular at first, Diem lost support through his own greed and corruption. He used his political power to increase his own and his family's wealth. A staunch Roman Catholic, Diem also persecuted members of the Buddhist clergy and ordered government troops to raid several Buddhist temples. After units of the South Vietnamese army attempted an overthrow, Diem cracked down on his political and religious opponents.

At the same time, North Vietnam's government began to wage guerrilla warfare

Photo by UPI/Bettmann

Cheering crowds lined the streets of Hanoi in 1954, when Viet Minh troops took possession of the city after eight years of fighting against the French.

This bridge across the Ben Hai River once was the dividing line between North Vietnam, which supported Communism, and South Vietnam, which had a democratic government. International agreements established the two separate nations in 1954 as a way to avoid a civil war. Despite the agreements, the Vietnam War broke out in the 1960s and lasted until 1975.

Photo by Rick Graetz, *Montana Magazine*

in South Vietnam. The DRV supported and trained the growing forces of the National Liberation Front (NLF). Also called the Viet Cong, this mobile group of South Vietnamese guerrilla fighters sought reunification of the country under the DRV's Communist regime.

By the early 1960s, the conflict in Vietnam—locally known as the Second Indochina War—had begun to gain international attention. Many countries, including the United States and the Soviet Union, viewed the war as an important regional struggle between the forces of democracy and Communism.

The U.S. government, headed by John F. Kennedy, believed the defeat of South Vietnam would bring all of Vietnam under Communist rule. To prevent that outcome, the Kennedy administration decided to give military aid to South Vietnam. Meanwhile, the United States disapproved of Diem's harsh government. Encouraged by U.S. officials, anti-Diem military officers overthrew him in November 1963. A military junta (ruling group) took over the government of South Vietnam.

Sensing a chance to weaken the new regime and to attract more southern support, North Vietnam and the NLF sent additional guerrilla forces into the south. Many of the units used the Ho Chi Minh Trail, a network of jungle paths that passed from North Vietnam through Laos and Cambodia to South Vietnam. Money, weapons, and training from China and the Soviet Union helped the North Vietnamese and the NLF to harass South Vietnam's troops.

In August 1964, a North Vietnamese gunboat attacked a U.S. ship patrolling the Gulf of Tonkin. The United States responded by increasing its own involvement in Vietnam. In 1965 President Lyndon B. Johnson, who had succeeded Kennedy, authorized air strikes against North Vietnam and sent the first U.S. combat troops into South Vietnam.

War and Withdrawal

Between 1965 and 1968, the Vietnam War was at its height. Neither side won decisive victories, and each used different fighting tactics. North Vietnam specialized in guerrilla warfare, while South Vietnam, backed by U.S. troops, used superior weapons to stage major offensives. At intervals, the United States heavily bombed Hanoi and Haiphong.

Courtesy of National Archives

Vietnam's civil war gradually drew in the armed forces of the United States. In 1968 two U.S. soldiers climbed a hill after landing at a secluded beach in the coastal lowlands.

During the Tet offensive in 1968, North Vietnam made an all-out effort to capture towns and villages in South Vietnam. (Tet is an important national celebration, and the attack broke a holiday truce.) North Vietnam believed the people in the countryside of South Vietnam would support the attack. Instead, North Vietnamese forces encountered strong resistance, and the fighting became the worst of the war. After a month of intense combat, the death toll was 40,000 for North Vietnam, 2,300 for the United States, and 1,100 for South Vietnam.

Despite its heavy losses, North Vietnam was determined to win the war. But the increasing cost in troops and supplies caused the U.S. government to reconsider its role. The Johnson administration looked for a way to withdraw from a conflict that was becoming hard to win in Vietnam and was increasingly unpopular in the United States. Richard M. Nixon, who succeeded Johnson in 1969, announced a gradual withdrawal of U.S. troops from Vietnam. At the same time, South Vietnam's armed forces would continue to receive U.S. training and weapons. Nixon also renewed international efforts to negotiate peace between the warring sides.

U.S. bombing of North Vietnam went on, destroying cities, industries, power plants, and roads. After the death of Ho Chi Minh in 1969 and after several more years of fighting, North Vietnam agreed to attend peace talks, which resulted in the Paris Agreement of January 27, 1973. The last U.S. troops left Vietnam two months later.

Despite the agreement, there was little break in the fighting for the people of Vietnam. In 1974 South Vietnam's government declared a renewal of the war. North Vietnam responded by launching a major offensive in early 1975. Without the support of U.S. troops, South Vietnam's forces collapsed, and North Vietnam achieved a total victory at the end of April. Within a year, the two parts of Vietnam—at war since 1945 and split since 1954—were united into the Socialist Republic of Vietnam.

Challenges of Reunification

The new nation faced severe challenges. Many parts of the country were in ruins. Battles and bombings had destroyed farmland, industries, and roads. The United States broke diplomatic relations with Vietnam and banned U.S. companies from trading and investing there.

These problems were in the hands of Le Duan, who had succeeded Ho Chi Minh as general secretary (leader) of the Communist party. Duan made efforts to extend Vietnam's authority in Southeast Asia. In 1978 the country invaded Cambodia and installed a pro-Vietnamese regime. The Vietnamese also supported a Communist takeover in Laos.

These actions angered Chinese officials, who did not want Vietnam to dominate Indochina. China invaded northern Vietnam in 1979 and cut off Chinese aid and imports. Moreover, to show its disapproval of Vietnam's invasion of Cambodia, the United States strengthened its trade embargo (ban) by preventing international agencies from sending aid to Vietnam. As a result of these economic restrictions, the nation drew closer to the Soviet Union, which became Vietnam's chief financial backer.

Despite Soviet support, Vietnam's economy continued to decline. Reunification had not solved the country's economic problems, nor had it eliminated the distinctions between the north and the south. The north was primarily an industrial center with an economy based on its plentiful energy resources and port facilities. The south was mainly agricultural, relying on productive farms and fertile soil. Both sections of the country were in need of immediate investment and modernization.

After the war, the government sought to unify the economies of the north and the south under a Communist system. Vietnamese officials collectivized southern farmland by combining small farms into large estates. The authorities also took over southern businesses, ending years of private ownership of industries. These actions put land and factories in the hands of the state, which now employed workers and set production targets for farms and industries.

ECONOMIC STRESS AND CHANGE

Throughout the 1970s and early 1980s, the Vietnamese government was determined to implement its economic plans, by force if necessary. Officials uprooted the populations of crowded southern cities—mainly Saigon, which had been renamed Ho Chi Minh City—and resettled them in new economic zones (NEZs). In these rural zones, little industrial or agricultural development had ever taken place.

The government used the NEZs not only to relieve urban crowding but also to break up South Vietnam's social structure. Communist authorities sent many southern intellectuals and professionals to reeducation camps. At these rural stations, southerners were both coerced through forced labor and encouraged through study to accept the Communist system. As a result of these harsh measures, thousands of people—many of them managers and skilled workers—fled the country in small boats, risking their lives for the chance to find a safer home and a better life.

Despite its bold attempts to restructure the economy, the government of Vietnam failed to provide enough supplies of food and basic consumer goods. As the economy worsened, the inflation rate reached 700 percent a year. In the early 1980s, the politicians who controlled the Vietnamese Communist party disagreed about how to achieve future goals. A conservative faction still pushed for centralized planning and public ownership of all farms and businesses. A liberal, reformist wing of the party thought that the government should change its strict economic policies.

Photo by Rick Graetz, *Montana Magazine*

Vietnamese army guards patrol a reeducation camp near Hanoi. After North Vietnam's troops overran South Vietnam in 1975, many southerners were taken to rural locations, where the authorities tried to instill Communist ideals in the people.

In 1985 rescuers from the United Nations *(right)* sped toward a crowded boat of Vietnamese refugees adrift in the South China Sea.

Le Duan achieved enough compromise to keep the party from splitting up over these differences. But after he died in July 1986, disputes erupted in the government. Eventually, Nguyen Van Linh, a reformist, became general secretary. He chose to work alongside Vo Van Kiet and Do Muoi, economic reformers in the Communist party.

Recent Events

Linh, Muoi, and Kiet introduced *doi moi* (meaning "renovation"), a package of economic reforms that allowed some private ownership of businesses. The policy also granted long-term leases to farmers so they would be encouraged to develop their land. The new leaders devalued the dong (the Vietnamese currency) to bring down the soaring inflation rate. They also sought more financial aid from the Soviet Union and the Communist nations of eastern Europe, which frequently traded and set up joint projects with Vietnam.

The attempts at reform improved the country's international standing. In 1989 Vietnam agreed to negotiate a settlement with Cambodia, and in 1991 the two countries signed a peace agreement that led to the withdrawal of Vietnamese troops. The following year, China began to mend its differences with Vietnam and gave its neighbor a small amount of economic aid. Vietnam's withdrawal from Cambodia gained the country an invitation to join the Association of Southeast Asian Nations (ASEAN). Vietnam's economy immediately benefited from increased trade with other ASEAN nations, such as Thailand, Singapore, and Malaysia.

In the early 1990s, growing political opposition and failing economies shook the Communist world. Many eastern European nations toppled their Communist governments, and the Soviet Union broke up. In Vietnam imports of oil, fertilizers, and raw materials from the former Soviet Union dropped sharply. Meanwhile, the continuing U.S. embargo slowed international investments in Vietnam and limited the country's trade with Japan and Europe. Despite these obstacles, Vietnamese leaders went ahead with their economic reform plans.

In 1991 Do Muoi succeeded Linh as general secretary of the Communist party, and Kiet became prime minister. They continued their efforts to forge closer ties with the non-Communist world, while keeping tight control over domestic politics. By early 1994, relations with the United States had improved, and the trade embargo was lifted. The change was partly because Vietnam was helping to locate the remains of missing U.S. soldiers who had served in Vietnam.

International banks, with U.S. approval, began lending money to Vietnam. This move encouraged Asian nations, such as South Korea, Japan, Hong Kong, and Taiwan, to set up businesses in Vietnam. Europeans and Americans also opened jointly operated factories in the country.

In 1995 the United States and Vietnam established diplomatic relations. The two nations slowly began working out details for a trade agreement. In exchange for full trading privileges, the United States has set forth several requirements. Vietnam must create an economic framework for foreign businesses, including lowered trade barriers and strong commercial laws. In addition to these reforms, the country must improve its human rights record.

In 1997 Vietnam pledged to repay money that the former South Vietnamese government borrowed from the United States. The promise strengthened ties between the two nations and improved Vietnam's position as a potential trade partner for the United States.

Several factors continue to hinder economic growth, however. Vietnam lacks a well-run banking system, which international investors need for their operations. The continuing influence of the country's

Funds from other Communist countries helped Vietnam to open factories that made bricks *(above)* **and straw mats** *(left).*

conservative, corrupt bureaucrats also stands in the way of progress.

As Vietnam works toward its economic and diplomatic goals, many of the nation's people are hopeful. The country's leadership, though resistant to political change, is eager for Vietnam to take its place among the thriving economies of Southeast Asia. The nation is making slow but steady progress toward a better future.

Government

Vietnam's government functions alongside the Communist party, whose most powerful institution is the Political Bureau. The dozen or more high-level leaders of the Political Bureau issue directives to the government. Every four to six years, the roughly 1.8 million members of the Com-

Photo by Reuters/Bettmann

In 1991 members of the Vietnamese Communist party elected Do Muoi to be the party's general secretary. He replaced Nguyen Van Linh, who was suffering from ill health. Muoi was reelected in 1996.

munist party attend meetings, where major policies are discussed and set. The general secretary is the party's top administrator.

Vietnam's highest legislative body is the National Assembly, which has 496 deputies who serve five-year terms. The National Assembly elects the Council of State, which appoints a prime minister. The prime minister runs the day-to-day operation of the government. The assembly also chooses a council of ministers, whose members head the various governmental departments and pass legislation.

The Communist party runs Vietnam's judicial system, whose highest tribunal is the Supreme People's Court. This court hears serious national cases, such as those for treason, and is the last court of appeals. People's Courts operate at the provincial, district, and city levels. Although judges at each division can send a case to a higher court, most make final rulings at their own particular levels.

Vietnam is divided into 37 provinces and the 3 independent city provinces of Hanoi, Ho Chi Minh City, and Haiphong. The elected provincial councils enjoy considerable independence from the central government. They have taken various approaches to economic development, political reforms, and other matters.

Photo © Nevada Wier

The Vietnamese flag—consisting of a yellow star on a red background—flies from a watchtower in Hanoi. The emblem was first used in 1955, after North Vietnam was established.

Vietnamese boys enjoy a joke outside their urban school. Only about 20 percent of the nation's population live in cities.

3) The People

Most of Vietnam's 75.1 million people live in the lowlands of the Red River and Mekong River deltas. The highest population density is in the Red River Delta, which holds as many as 1,000 people per square mile. In Hanoi density reaches 3,640 people per square mile. The Mekong Delta has a lower density but a larger total population.

Vietnam's population is growing at a fast annual rate of 1.6 percent, a pace that will double the country's population within 43 years. The Vietnamese government, which wants to slow the growth rate, has yet to come up with a workable family-planning program. Couples continue to marry young and to have four or five children. Family-planning supplies are available to about half of all married couples.

Eighty percent of the Vietnamese dwell in rural areas, mostly in small villages.

To relieve urban crowding, a government resettlement program has moved more than five million people to NEZs in the Central Highlands, in the coastal lowlands, and on nearby islands.

Most rural families live in thatched dwellings and work on collectivized or private farms. Small gardens supply the families with additional food. Few rural areas have electricity or public water supplies, and most families must carry water from nearby streams. These conditions give couples more reasons to have several children, who can share the work of farming the land and maintaining the home.

Most city dwellers live in small apartments, many of which house three genera-
tions of a single family. Furniture is sparse in most homes, and at mealtimes families traditionally sit on the floor around a small table. Wood, thatch, and bamboo are popular building materials for homes in the south, where the weather is warm year-round. In the north, houses of stone protect residents from cooler temperatures and seasonal storms.

Ethnic Mixture

Nearly 90 percent of Vietnam's citizens are ethnic Vietnamese who are descendants of the early peoples of the Red River Delta. Ethnic Vietnamese dominate the nation's administration and industry. Most senior

An elderly ethnic Vietnamese stands in the doorway of his home.

Near Hanoi, a young mother holds her toddler. A Vietnamese woman of childbearing age (15 to 49) has an average of four children during her lifetime.

People of the Ede national minority enlarge their long houses by adding sections to the front and the back. By tradition, after females in the family get married, they and their spouses reside with her parents. Each pair of newlyweds has its own private living space. Dining and cooking areas are shared by all family members.

officials of the Communist party and of the government come from this group. Ethnic Vietnamese also hold most of the country's managerial jobs.

One reminder of the U.S. presence in southern Vietnam is the many Amerasians in Saigon. These children, the offspring of U.S. soldiers and ethnic Vietnamese women, have not been accepted into Vietnamese society and often live on the streets as best they can.

NATIONAL MINORITIES

About 12 percent of Vietnam's population belong to 53 other ethnic groups, officially called national minorities. Most have their historic origins in Southeast Asia or southern China. Many live in remote areas that have been the last to receive educational and health benefits.

In the mountains of northern Vietnam, the largest ethnic groups are the Tai (2,000,000), the Muong (550,000), the Hmong Meo (200,000), and the Zao (200,000). Tai speech is similar to the language spoken in Thailand, while the Muong language is closely related to Vietnamese. People from the Hmong Meo and Zao groups speak Sino-Tibetan dialects that are rooted in China.

Numerous ethnic communities, whom the French collectively called Montagnards (mountain people), populate the Central Highlands. These groups total about one million people and are very diverse in languages, customs, and appearance. The most numerous are the Jarai (150,000), the Ede (100,000), and the Bahnar (100,000). The majority of Montagnards are nomadic farmers. Some Montagnard groups have earned

Photo by Rick Graetz, *Montana Magazine*

These Cham women carry crossed poles that are attached to fine nets for catching fish.

Photo © Nevada Wier

A young member of the Tai minority holds onto the hands of his parents.

a reputation for skill in battle and were recruited to fight against North Vietnam during the war.

Also living in the Central Highlands are about 100,000 Cham, whose kingdom of Champa dominated central Vietnam until the late 1400s. After the Cham retreated to the highlands, they converted to the Islamic faith. Their culture was also greatly influenced by India and its Hindu beliefs, which many Cham still honor.

In southern Vietnam, the largest ethnic minority is the Khmer, who number about 700,000. The main ethnic group in Cambodia, the Khmer are closely related to the Mon people of Myanmar. The Khmer Empire once extended across the southern part of Southeast Asia and included all

Photo © Tovya Wager/Asian Pacific Adventures

This Hmong Meo mother and daughter live in the hills of Son La province. This area borders Laos, where many other Hmong also make their homes.

During the colonial era, the French put up this distance marker along the route to Hanoi. The stone shows the accented Latin alphabet introduced by the French. Previously, the Vietnamese had only used Chinese characters to write their language.

of the Mekong Delta. Most Vietnamese Khmer live west of Saigon and south of the Mekong River.

At least 500,000 ethnic Chinese, called Hoa, also live in the lowlands of southern Vietnam. In the early twentieth century, the Chinese dominated trade and banking, but many Vietnamese distrusted them. After the Communists reunified the nation, Vietnam's Chinese population became the target of persecution. As a result, thousands of Hoa fled to China in small boats, and many died before reaching their destination.

Language and Literature

Vietnam's language reflects the complex history of its people. Ninety percent of the words used in everyday speech are identical to words in Mon-Khmer, the language family of Cambodia. Other Vietnamese words come from the Thai language. Many administrative, technical, and literary terms in Vietnamese are of Chinese origin.

For centuries Vietnamese scholars used the Chinese language and writing system. Later they developed *chu nom,* a form of writing that adapted Chinese ideograms (pictorial forms) to express Vietnamese words. The use of ideograms declined after the 1600s, when a Catholic missionary developed *quoc ngu,* an alphabet that employs Latin letters and that shows pronunciation with accent marks. Vietnamese authors wrote in chu nom until the colonial era, when Vietnamese literature adopted quoc ngu.

The oldest Vietnamese writings are folk tales meant to be recited. Some of these fables relate the adventures of legendary heroes. Others offer explanations of natural wonders, such as how the water buffalo got its wrinkled skin.

Spoken Vietnamese lends itself well to poetry, which was the literary form preferred in past centuries. The first major collections of poems were written by court officials and Buddhist monks in the 1100s, after Vietnam gained its independence from China. During the Tran dynasty, historical writings became important. One of the most notable collections is *Historical Memoirs of the Great Viet,* a long work by Le Van Huu.

Probably the most famous piece of Vietnamese literature is *Kim Van Kieu* (The Tale of Kieu), a 3,250-verse poem written by Nguyen Du (1765–1820). This romantic work describes the painful struggles of a beautiful girl named Thuy Kieu. Many Vietnamese can recite whole sections of the poem from memory and sometimes consult passages to help solve personal problems.

Novels, short stories, essays, and dramas became important literary forms in Vietnam in the twentieth century. After 1975, to stop criticism of Communism, the Vietnamese government placed strict controls on the content of published works. Since 1989 officials have allowed writers much more freedom.

One of the best-selling modern writers is Nguyen Manh Tuan, whose novels often criticize the Communist party. Thich Nhat

In *The Tale of Kieu,* written by the Vietnamese author Nguyen Du, the heroine falls in love with Tu Hai *(right),* who dies trying to comfort and protect her.

Independent Picture Service

Hanh, a Buddhist monk, writes popular poems, novels, and folk tales. Some of his works, such as *A Taste of Earth* and *Hermitage among the Sleeping Clouds,* have been translated into English.

The Arts

Vietnam has distinct styles in music and folk arts. Classical Vietnamese music is played on five instruments, which musicians and composers call "the five perfects." The *nhi,* similar to a mandolin, has 2 strings, and the *dan tranh,* a type of zither, has 16 strings. The *dan nguyet* resembles a long-necked guitar. The *dan tam* and *ty* are also guitarlike instruments, with 3 and 4 strings, respectively.

Photo © William Short

Plants, scenes of dragons, and urns filled with burning incense (perfumed sticks) decorate a temple in Hanoi.

42

Courtesy of Linda James

Water puppetry *(above)* **is a favorite art form in northern Vietnam. A pond acts as the stage, with the audience sitting at the edge of the water. From a separate room, puppeteers control the wooden figures by wires and strings that are hidden beneath the surface. Music is another popular form of artistic expression in the country. Traditional instruments include the** *ty (below),* **a four-stringed guitar shaped like a pear.**

Vietnam's festival tunes, love songs, and lullabies are usually sung without accompaniment. Each region of the country and each ethnic group has its own folk melodies. The sad songs of the south, for example, show influences from Champa and India. The boat tunes of Hue, in central Vietnam, glorify heroes of the past.

Vietnamese popular theater combines singing and instrumental music with poetry, dance, and mime. Performers often use satirical folk songs to criticize the government. Classical theater, based on Chinese opera, came to Vietnam in the thirteenth century. In these plays, the actors use makeup colors to represent traits such as courage or faithfulness. Six musicians accompany each drama.

Puppet theater is a traditional favorite in Vietnam, where a unique form of the art—water puppetry—developed centuries ago. The puppeteers control wooden figures with rods and strings hidden beneath

Photo from Maurice Durand Collection of Vietnamese Art, Yale University Library

Photo © Nevada Wier

Artists hand paint a lacquered box *(left)* **and ceramic elephants** *(below).*

Photo by Rick Graetz, *Montana Magazine*

the water. As the forms walk gracefully on water, they are surrounded by a stage of sky, trees, and clouds.

Vietnamese artisans began making shiny lacquerware objects in the 1400s. Traditionally, lacquer came from the sap of *son* trees. Artists put on the lacquer in separate coats over wooden objects decorated with gold, inlaid pearl, or other materials. Modern craftspeople apply a synthetic resin to produce lacquerware.

The Chinese taught the Vietnamese how to make porcelain and other ceramics. Tiles with Chinese designs became a widely used building decoration in the eleventh century. During the Le and Tran dynasties, the Vietnamese created their own distinctive glazes and earthenware designs.

Religion

The religion of Buddhism spread to Vietnam from China and India as early as the second century A.D. The Chinese form, called Mahayana Buddhism, dominated northern Vietnam. The Indian style, Theravada Buddhism, influenced central and southern Vietnam. Both forms are based on the teachings of the Buddha (a title meaning "enlightened one"), an Indian prince who lived in the sixth century B.C. Stressing good behavior and moral duties, Buddhism encourages believers to seek perfection through self-knowledge.

Although Buddhism became Vietnam's official religion in the 1100s, for centuries scholars and members of the royal court were the only people who followed the faith. Most Vietnamese maintained their ancient beliefs, which included worship of their ancestors and respect for a powerful spirit world.

Two religious sects developed in southern Vietnam in the early twentieth century. A faith healer founded Hoa Hao, a reformed Buddhist group that now claims about two million members. This sect emphasizes simplicity of worship and a direct relationship between the individual and the supreme being. The Cao Dai religious sect, which combines several different Asian and European philosophies, also has about two million followers.

About 10 percent of Vietnamese are Roman Catholic, a faith brought by French missionaries in the 1600s. In 1954, after the country was divided, thousands of North Vietnamese Catholics fled to South Vietnam to avoid harassment. In South Vietnam, meanwhile, President Ngo Dinh Diem, a strong Catholic, persecuted Buddhists and other non-Catholics. Soon after the Communist victory of 1975, the government restricted activities of Catholics and Buddhists throughout Vietnam. More recently Buddhist temples and Catholic churches have been allowed to hold services and to teach.

This large statue of the Buddha, the founder of the Buddhist religion, dominates a flight of steps in Nha Trang.

Monks of the Cao Dai sect kneel on the floor of their main temple in Tay Ninh province, southern Vietnam.

Vietnam also contains Protestants and Muslims (followers of the Islamic religion). Most of the 200,000 Protestants are Montagnards of the Central Highlands. About 180,000 people, mainly Khmer and Cham, follow Islam.

Education

The Vietnamese have long valued education as a means to get better jobs and a higher rank in society. For centuries, however, education was within reach of only the richest Vietnamese families. Since the 1950s, schooling has been available to everyone, and attendance at public schools has been high. Although Vietnam does not have enough teachers, books, and school buildings, the country's literacy rate has risen to 88 percent.

French colonial officials introduced a European educational system, in which children begin primary school at the age of six. After seven years, students can enter secondary school for general education or vocational training. In the early 1990s, about 40 percent of primary-school graduates went on to secondary school.

Graduates of secondary schools have access to more than 100 universities, technical colleges, and specialized schools in Vietnam. In the early 1990s, these institutions had a total enrollment of about 130,000 students. The country's largest universities are in Hue, Hanoi, and Ho Chi Minh City.

The eleventh-century Temple of Literature in Hanoi is Vietnam's oldest school, where Confucian scholars instilled in their wealthy students respect for literature and learning.

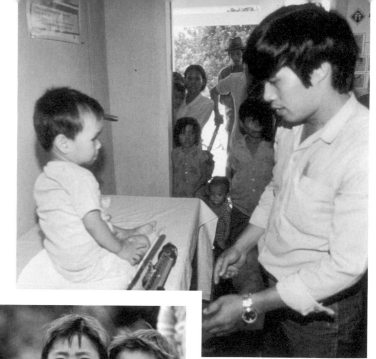

A doctor from the Ministry of Health weighs a young patient to see if the child's weight is right for his age. Many Vietnamese children—as well as adults—suffer from malnutrition.

Courtesy of Peyton Johnson/FAO

Courtesy of Save the Children

About 40 percent of Vietnam's total population is younger than 15 years of age.

Health

Decades of war and periodic famines have taken a toll on the health of the Vietnamese, and improving health care is a national priority. The government trains medical personnel, administers hospitals, distributes medicines, and coordinates medical research.

The Vietnamese receive free medical care, and almost every village has a health center staffed by part-time health workers. Patients who need more specialized treatment can go to district or urban health facilities. Shortages of drugs and medical equipment, however, limit the effectiveness of some types of treatment.

The infant mortality rate—the number of babies who die within their first year—is 38 in every 1,000 live births. This figure is lower than the average for Southeast Asia. Life expectancy at birth is 67 years, which is also better than average for the region.

Among the diseases that still afflict the Vietnamese are bubonic plague and cholera. Doctors have made progress in controlling tuberculosis, leprosy, malaria, and trachoma, which causes blindness. Despite government efforts to improve public health, widespread malnutrition makes the population susceptible to illness. Mothers, most of whom must work outside the

47

In Ho Chi Minh City, a wreath maker fashions flowers into colorful funeral offerings.

Boys in Hanoi admire long strings of pink firecrackers that will be set off during Tet, Vietnam's New Year's festival.

The burning of fireworks creates a smoky atmosphere during the Dong Ky Fireworks Festival, when competitions choose the best displays.

48

home, usually stop breast-feeding their babies after three months. Instead of milk, children eat a thin rice soup that lacks important nutrients. In recent years, about 20 percent of Vietnamese babies have been born with birth defects. These defects may be linked to chemicals sprayed on forested areas during the Vietnam War.

Festivals and Food

The people of Vietnam celebrate many religious and nonreligious occasions. The most important religious festival is Tet, which falls in late January or early February and marks the arrival of spring and the new year. The Vietnamese follow special rituals for each day of Tet to ensure good luck for the coming year.

Other holidays include Liberation Day on April 30, which marks the 1975 surrender of South Vietnam to North Vietnam. In place of birthdays, the Vietnamese honor their deceased relatives on the anniversary of death, when the family places gifts and food in temples and homes. People throughout the nation mark the anniversary of Ho Chi Minh's death, for example, on September 2.

Food has an important place not only during Vietnamese festivals but also in daily life. Although plain rice is their dietary staple, the Vietnamese combine different vegetables, fruits, fish, and meats in a cuisine of great variety. A favorite seasoning is *nuoc mam,* a liquid made from heavily salted fish that have fermented in large vats for months. Cooks combine nuoc mam with sugar, lime juice, vinegar, red pepper flakes, shallots, garlic, and carrots to make *nuoc cham,* a sauce served at almost every meal.

Courtesy of Peyton Johnson/FAO

A group of Cham Muslims (followers of the Islamic religion) observe a holy day with a variety of foods.

During a Buddhist festival, fruits and vegetables crowd the floor of a temple in Ha Bac province.

Popular dishes include filleted fish slices broiled over charcoal and frog meat soaked in a thin batter and fried in oil. *Pho,* one of many Vietnamese noodle soups, is popular for breakfast. *Cha gio,* a side dish, is made from thin rice paper filled with finely chopped pork, crab, noodles, mushrooms, eggs, and onions. The ingredients are packed into a tight roll and deep fried. A special seasonal treat often served during Tet is *banh-chung*—square cakes made of rice, yellow beans, pork, scallions, and spices. Before serving it, cooks wrap the mixture in banana leaves and boil it for eight hours.

In preparation for the celebration of Tet, a family works together to make *banh-chung,* or bean cakes.

A pair of cyclo drivers wait for passengers in Hanoi. The rider relaxes in the canopied seat while the driver, who sits behind the passenger, pedals the vehicle.

4) The Economy

After the fighting ended in 1975, Vietnam faced the difficult task of rebuilding its war-damaged economy. To achieve this goal, the Communist government sought to integrate the economy of the south with that of the north. Another priority was to move the south from a free-market economic system to a centrally planned one.

Under a Communist approach, the government makes all privately owned land, banks, factories, and businesses the property of the state. This step, called nationalization, allows government officials to control wages and prices and to set production quotas (goals) for industries and farms. By setting quotas, Vietnamese leaders hoped to increase crop yields and the output of consumer goods.

With large amounts of financial aid from the Soviet Union, the Vietnamese

51

After the Vietnam War ended in 1975, workers in damaged areas filled bomb craters *(above)* **and stepped up production in textile mills** *(below).*

government began projects to expand agriculture, to reconstruct roads, and to rebuild factories. To ease the economic burden on cities, the plans included shifting about five million people from urban areas to new economic zones (NEZs). In addition, southern farmland was organized into state-owned collectives.

By the late 1980s, Vietnam's leaders realized these plans were not achieving the expected growth. Harvests were low, and consumer goods were still in short supply. In response to these conditions, the government introduced the economic reforms contained in doi moi. This policy relaxed the strict laws governing landownership and provided incentives to encourage investors to start new enterprises. Although these changes stimulated some economic activity, other problems arose.

In 1991 the Soviet Union, one of Vietnam's main sources of funding and im-

A carpenter at a veteran's hospital in Ho Chi Minh City makes final measurements on an artificial leg. According to some estimates, three million Vietnamese were wounded in the fighting that took place in the 1960s and 1970s.

ports, broke up. This event caused a sharp drop in financial aid and shortages of manufactured items and raw materials. Vietnam's unemployment rate started to climb. At the same time, the 19-year U.S. embargo on trade with Vietnam curbed investment and imports.

In 1994, however, the U.S. government lifted the embargo to give U.S. firms access to the growing Vietnamese economy. Hundreds of small and large businesses have sprung up in the major cities. Farmers' markets display a wide variety of once-scarce fruits and vegetables. Foreign banks and manufacturing firms have set up offices in Vietnam. These outside groups will be hiring from local workers who are motivated and educated—advantages that may speed up the nation's economic recovery.

Agriculture

After the war and before reform policies were in place, Vietnam had trouble feeding its people. Government policies set the

The Soviet Union, once Vietnam's main source of foreign aid, funded the building of this mausoleum (above-ground tomb) to house the body of Ho Chi Minh, who died in 1969.

53

price of rice and limited the profit of farmers. Famines occurred when rice harvests were poor or when tropical storms damaged fields. The doi moi reforms—which included the removal of price controls—gave farmers reasons to increase their crop yields. As a result, by 1989 Vietnam was able to feed its own population and had become the world's third largest rice exporter, after the United States and Thailand.

Farming employs about 65 percent of Vietnam's labor force, and rice is the most important crop. The richest soils for rice cultivation are in the Mekong Delta. More than half of Vietnam's rice fields produce two crops each year. By irrigating, some farmers in the Red River Delta can grow three crops annually. High-yield rice seeds also have dramatically increased the volume of the rice crop. Farm fertilizers, once imported from the Soviet Union, have fur-

Photo © Tovya Wager/Asian Pacific Adventures

Lush rice fields in northern Vietnam *(left)* **can yield three crops in a single year. Workers** *(below left)* **use a simple tool to separate the grains of rice from the stalks. A farmer in southern Vietnam** *(below right)* **carefully prepares a clump of rice seedlings for planting.**

Courtesy of Save the Children

Photo © Nevada Wier

Photo © Tovya Wager/Asian Pacific Adventures

Photo © Nevada Wier

A laborer *(above left)* **on a cash-crop farming estate picks tea leaves by hand. Many Vietnamese farmers raise ducks** *(above right)* **as sources of food and use water buffalo** *(right)* **as work animals.**

Photo © Nevada Wier

ther boosted yields. To replace foreign-made fertilizers, Vietnamese farmers are now experimenting with natural treatments that improve the soil without using chemicals.

Many family-run and state-run farms grow non-grain crops—principally corn, beans, sweet potatoes, and cassavas. Smaller holdings produce citrus fruits, bananas, papayas, coconuts, and mangoes. The gov-ernment encourages the cultivation of these secondary crops to avoid the famines that have occurred when rice harvests have been poor. Nevertheless, as rice yields have improved, the production of secondary crops has fallen.

Established during the colonial era, estates devoted to cash-crop farming cultivate peanuts, jute, soybeans, tobac-co, rubber trees, tea plants, and coffee

Courtesy of Peyton Johnson/FAO

A villager casts a net to harvest shrimp from a communal shrimp and fish pond.

shrubs. Money earned from the export of these products allows Vietnam to import needed goods, such as fuels, machinery, and raw materials.

By setting aside public land for grazing, the government is promoting the breeding of more cattle and water buffalo, which are valued work animals. Larger livestock herds produce a greater supply of manure, which can sometimes substitute for scarce fertilizers. Vietnamese farmers also raise pigs and poultry for food and for sale.

Fishing and Forestry

The Vietnamese government has long encouraged the expansion of the fishing industry, but growth has been slow. One cause of the lack of progress was the loss of small fishing boats in the 1970s and 1980s, when many Vietnamese used them to flee the country.

Vietnam's principal fishing areas lie off the coastal lowlands in the South China Sea, where the government has claimed a fishing zone of more than 350,000 square miles. Annual catches of crab, shrimp, lobster, squid, and mackerel usually total around one million tons.

During the Vietnam War, bombing and chemical spraying destroyed vast stretches of untouched forests. The clearing of land by farmers and the logging of trees to provide fuel has also threatened woodlands.

An intensive reforestation project in the 1980s established hardy, fast-growing eucalyptus and acacia trees, whose shade protects more valuable hardwoods that mature slowly. Soldiers, schoolchildren, and teenagers planted hundreds of millions of trees, blanketing thousands of acres of once-deforested land. If managed well, Vietnam's forests have the potential to provide building material for markets in Japan, Australia, and Thailand.

As the Vietnamese population goes up, there is a growing need for wood as a cooking fuel. Stands of eucalyptus planted in the 1980s are already being harvested to provide wood. Some Vietnamese activists are urging the replanting of trees in the Mekong Delta to meet future demand.

Manufacturing and Trade

Although the French and the Japanese established a few industries in Vietnam, manufacturing became more important after the country gained its independence. Private businesses in South Vietnam made consumer goods, while government-run factories in North Vietnam turned out heavy machinery. In the 1980s, Soviet aid helped to build a battery factory, a flour mill, a tea-processing operation, and a cement plant in the north. A rubber company and several machine and tool repair facilities opened in southern Vietnam.

Despite a growing manufacturing sector, Vietnam was still importing most consumer goods in the early 1990s. Some arrived as gifts from overseas relatives.

Young workers gently place tree seedlings in boxes at a nursery near the city of Da Lat in south central Vietnam. Crews then plant the seedlings in the surrounding hillsides, which have lost much of their natural tree cover.

Many products smuggled from Thailand ended up on Vietnam's thriving "black market." People in northern Vietnam crossed the border into China with farm produce and returned with scarce manufactured items.

Factories that process agricultural products, such as tea and rubber, are built near the areas in which the crops are raised. Small-scale factories make farm tools, bicycles, and other cheap goods. The production of paper, bricks, glass, and textiles is growing, but a lack of raw materials has slowed the manufacture of cement and fertilizer. The country's only oil refinery sends its output to Japan and Singapore, but the small amount of exported petroleum brings limited income to Vietnam.

To stimulate manufacturing, Vietnam actively seeks outside investors. Since 1987 the government has allowed domestic companies to undertake joint projects

Photo © Nevada Wier

Photo © Nevada Wier

At a factory in Thuan Hai province, a technician *(top)* **monitors vats of** *nuoc mam,* **the fish sauce that is a staple part of the Vietnamese diet. Sorting shrimp is the job of this assembly line** *(above)* **at a frozen food company in Ho Chi Minh City.**

Photo © Nevada Wier

(Above) Foreign consumer goods—including canned beverages—have begun to appear throughout Vietnam since the government loosened restrictions on trade. (Below) The Belgian company Petrofina is exploring for oil in the waters just southwest of Vietnam.

Courtesy of Petrofina

with foreign firms and has encouraged foreign-owned companies to set up plants in Vietnam. Foreign investment in the country has risen dramatically in the last few years, and companies from all over the world have started ventures with Vietnamese partners. The growing number of businesses has created a need for factories and office buildings, sparking an increase in construction work. The new firms have also begun to supply more of the consumer goods that Vietnamese citizens are eager, and increasingly able, to purchase.

Since the fall of the Soviet Union, Japan has become Vietnam's principal trading partner. Other active partners are Thailand, Singapore, and Malaysia—all members of ASEAN. Vietnam mainly exports agricultural products, such as rice, coffee, tea, and rubber. The country's chief imports are petroleum, steel, vehicles, machinery, fertilizers, and medicines.

Energy and Mining

Coal, hydroelectric installations, and petroleum are Vietnam's primary sources of domestic energy. In the late 1800s, the French began extracting Vietnam's coal to fuel their merchant fleet, and coal remains one of the country's most important exports. Reserves in northern Vietnam are sizable, and economic planners would like to increase production. A lack of money to invest in new mining equipment has hampered this goal, however.

With the help of Soviet funds and technology, Vietnam expanded its energy production in the late 1980s and early 1990s. The government opened several new hydroelectric plants, including a huge facility in northern Vietnam. Additional plants, such as a thermal station in Pha Lai and a nuclear reactor in Da Lat, have also contributed to the increase.

The Soviets aided the Vietnamese in developing their oil and natural gas industries. In 1986 drilling began in a large oil field in the South China Sea. Since then, more fields have been discovered in the region. Vietnam now allows companies from Britain, India, Belgium, Canada, and Australia to drill for oil in offshore waters. Payments from these foreign oil contracts will significantly boost Vietnam's economy.

The hills of northern Vietnam contain small amounts of many minerals, which have been tapped by French, Japanese, and Soviet companies. West of Cao Bang are deposits of tin and tungsten, both of which Vietnam extracts and exports. Northern Vietnam also provides iron ore and has large reserves of zinc. The country's other mineral resources include antimony, chromium, bauxite, pyrite, and phosphates.

Transportation

The lack of a good transportation network hampers Vietnam's efforts to improve its economy. The main railway lines run be-

Photo by Rick Graetz, *Montana Magazine*

Coal yards near Ha Long Bay provide local people with fuel for home use.

Courtesy of CIDA/Cindy Andrew

Vans heavily laden with goods and personal belongings rumble along a roughly paved road.

North of Haiphong, people on foot and on bicycles board a ferry that crosses the Red River.

tween Hanoi and Ho Chi Minh City, between Haiphong and Yunnan, China, and between Hanoi and Guangxi, China. Although most of these lines have been rebuilt since the Vietnam War, many sections still need to be modernized. For example, a serious bottleneck occurs at the Hai Van Pass north of Da Nang. This spot is the only place for freight trains to pass between the southern and northern parts of the country.

Vietnam's road system is unable to handle a rising volume of car and truck traffic. The two-lane national artery between Hanoi and Ho Chi Minh City is in disrepair, as is the 60-mile road between Hanoi and Haiphong. Vietnamese soldiers have widened the famed Ho Chi Minh Trail, now called the Truong Son Highway, so that it can accommodate heavy vehicles. Although U.S. bombing destroyed many of the country's roads, bridges, and ports, the U.S. military also constructed new transportation routes. The largest U.S.-built highway links Ho Chi Minh City and Bien Hoa.

Ho Chi Minh City is the principal port of southern Vietnam. In the north, the government is updating and enlarging Haiphong's crowded docks. In south central Vietnam, timber exporters use the ports of Qui Nhon and Nha Trang, both of which the government plans to modernize.

Asian and European airlines fly into Tan Son Nhut, near Ho Chi Minh City, as well as into a new airport that opened outside of Hanoi. Vietnam Airlines, the national carrier, uses mostly old Soviet aircraft. The U.S. embargo once prevented planes produced with U.S. technology from being sold to Vietnam. The country's airline now has a few Boeing 737s in its fleet.

Tourism

Despite poor road, rail, and air links, travelers are flocking to Vietnam. Some are businesspeople investigating trade and manufacturing opportunities. Others are Vietnamese-born foreigners—called Viet Kieu—who come to see relatives or to

A Vietnamese veteran of the Vietnam War *(above left)* **leads tourists through the Cu Chi tunnels. Lacquerware and portraits of Ho Chi Minh** *(above right)* **dominate a souvenir stand in Nha Trang. The cruise ship** *Aurora I (left)* **makes its way through Ha Long Bay in northern Vietnam.**

invest in local businesses. A number of tourists are Vietnam War veterans from the United States who revisit old battlefields. In need of foreign currency, the Vietnamese government welcomes them all. The hotel industry has boomed with the wave of visitors. Cafes, nightclubs, and restaurants have reopened, especially in Ho Chi Minh City and Hanoi.

Guided by former soldiers, tourists can explore the Cu Chi tunnels, a 120-mile underground network of passageways used by the NLF to infiltrate South Vietnam. Ancient temples, Buddhist shrines, and Champa ruins draw people interested in Vietnam's earlier history. Mountain resorts, such as Da Lat, offer cool temperatures and breathtaking scenery. Broad beaches, especially near Da Nang and Nha Trang, attract foreign guests as well as Vietnamese vacationers. In Hanoi visitors can enjoy the city's French-colonial architecture or view the embalmed remains of Ho Chi Minh in a huge, Soviet-built mausoleum. Hue presents historic tombs and buildings from the period of Vietnam's last independent emperors.

The Future

Although the standard of living in Vietnam remained very low in the early 1990s, the economy was showing signs of recovery. New directions taken by Vietnam's leaders have drawn foreign companies to the country. Corporations from Asia and Europe have set up factories to produce a wide range of consumer goods. Billboards in Hanoi and Ho Chi Minh City advertise the latest in electronics equipment. Small businesses and bustling farmers' markets crowd city streets. Nevertheless, in both parts of the country, the continuing prob-lem of corruption, bureaucratic delays, and a poor transportation network pose obstacles to progress.

Vietnam's biggest challenge, however, is to balance its economic goals with its political ideals. The Communist government must decide how much, and how quickly, to allow free competition in the country. Vietnam needs the economic growth that foreign investment and trade can provide, and overseas businesses are willing to establish long-term operations in a market that shows enormous promise. Yet the nation's leaders hesitate to surrender control over Vietnam's economy and resources. Officials also fear that social problems will spread along with capitalism. The next decade will show whether or not Vietnam can realize its economic potential while retaining the degree of government control it has had in the past.

Photo © Nevada Wier

A sign painter in Hanoi finishes an advertisement for videos, which are becoming more common in urban Vietnamese homes, hotels, and businesses.

Index

Agriculture, 5–6, 9–10, 21, 28, 33–34, 38, 52–56. *See also* Livestock; Rice
Amerasians, 39
Ancient kingdoms, 20–22
Annam, 26–27, 29
Annamite Chain. *See* Truong Son Mountains
Architecture, 16–17, 62–63
Arts, 42–44
Association of Southeast Asian Nations (ASEAN), 34, 59
An Lac kingdom, 21
Australia, 57, 59–60
Bao Dai, 30
Belgium, 59–60, 63
Ben Hai River, 10, 30–31
Britain, 29, 60
Buddhism, 22–23. 30, 44–45
Burma. *See* Myanmar
Cambodia, 8, 10, 15, 20, 25–26, 28, 31–34, 40–41, 63
Canada, 60
Cao Dai sect, 45
Central Highlands, 10–11, 13, 28, 38–40, 46
Cham, 20, 23, 40, 46
Champa, kingdom of, 19, 23–24, 40, 43
China, 5, 8, 10, 21–25, 29, 31, 33–34, 39, 41, 44, 58
Christianity, 25–26
Cities. 15–19. *See also* Dat Lat; Da Nang; Haiphong; Hanoi; Ho Chi Minh City; Hue; Saigon
Civil war, 6, 29–32
Climate, 11–13
Coal, 14, 28, 60
Cochin China, 26–27, 29
Colonization, 26–30
Communist party, 6–7, 28–36, 45, 51
Confucianism, 21–24, 46
Da Lat, 14, 57, 60, 62
Da Nang, 12, 15, 19, 26, 62
Dai Viet (Greater Viet), 22–24
Deforestation, 13–14, 56
Dien Bien Phu, 29
Do Muoi, 34–36
Dong-son period, 20–21
Economy, 7, 16–17, 33–34, 51–63
Education, 39, 41, 46
Energy, 19, 60
Ethnic mixture, 38–41
Ethnic Vietnamese, 38–39
Europe, 25, 35, 63
Exports, 15, 19, 25, 28, 54–56, 58–60, 63
Family planning, 37–38
Fauna, 13–14
Festivals, 48–50
First Indochina War, 29–30
Fishing, 3, 10, 15, 19, 40, 56
Flora, 13–14
Food, 2, 18, 49–50
Foreign investment, 17, 35–36, 52–53, 58–59
Forestry, 9, 13–15, 56–57
France, 6, 15–16, 26–30, 45, 60, 63
Gia Long, Emperor, 19, 26
Government, 36
Haiphong, 14–15, 18–19, 31, 36, 59, 61

Ha Long Bay, 8, 60, 62
Hanoi, 7–8, 10–11, 14–15, 17–18, 24, 30–31, 33, 36–37, 42, 46, 48, 51, 61–63
Health, 7, 39, 47, 49
History, 5–7, 20–36
divided Vietnam, 30–32
early kingdoms, 20–26
French control, 26–30
Indochina wars, 29–32
reunification, 32–36
Hoa Hao, 45
Ho Chi Minh, 15, 18, 28–30, 32, 49, 53, 62–63
Ho Chi Minh City, 11, 15–17, 33, 36, 46, 48, 53, 58–59, 61–63. *See also* Saigon
Ho Chi Minh Trail, 31, 61
Hong Kong, 35, 59
Housing, 38
Hue, 2, 11, 15, 17, 19, 22, 26, 43, 46, 63
Hydroelectric power, 19, 60
Imports, 19, 34, 56–57, 59, 63
Independence, 5–6, 22, 29–30
India, 43–44, 59–60
Indochinese Communist party (ICP), 29
Indochinese Peninsula, 8, 21, 24, 29
Indochinese Union, 26, 28–29
Industry, 33, 35, 57–59
Inflation, 33–34
Irrigation, 20–21, 28, 54
Islam, 46
Japan, 6, 18, 25, 29, 35, 57–60
Khmer, 20, 40, 46
Khmer Empire, 15, 25, 40
Lacquerware, 44, 62
Languages, 39, 41
Laos, 8, 10, 19, 26, 31–32, 40
Le Duan, 32–34
Le dynasty, 23–24, 44
Le Loi, 24
Le Thanh Tong, 24
Literature, 2–25, 41–42
Livestock, 14, 55–56
Ly dynasty, 17, 22
Mac Dang Dung, 24
Malaysia, 34, 59
Manufacturing, 35, 52, 57–59, 61
Maps and charts, 4, 12, 16, 27
Mekong River, 10, 41
Mekong River Delta, 5, 9–10, 15, 20, 24–26, 28, 37, 41, 54, 57
Minerals and mining, 14–15, 28, 60
Minorities. *See* National Minorities
Missionaries, 25–26, 45
Mongols, 23
Monsoons, 11–12
Montagnards, 39–40, 46
Music, 42–43
Myanmar, 10, 40
Nam Viet, 21–22
Nationalization, 51
National Liberation Front, 31, 62
National Minorities, 39–41. *See also* Cham; Khmer; Montagnards
Natural resources, 14–15, 28

New economic zones (NEZs), 33, 38, 52
Ngo Dinh Diem, 30–31, 45
Ngo Quyen, 22
Nguyen dynasty, 24–26
Nguyen Phuc Anh, 26
Nguyen Van Linh, 34
Nha Trang, 15, 19, 24, 45, 61–62
North Vietnam, 6, 29, 30 33, 49
Oil, 7, 15, 34, 58 60, 63
Paracel Islands, 8
Paris Agreement, 32
People, 37–50
celebrations, 48–50
ethnic mixture, 38–41
housing, 38 literacy, 46
national minorities. 39–41
Population, 5, 37
Ports, 18–19, 61
Protestants, 46
Railways, 60–61
Rainfall, 11–13
Red River, 9–10, 17, 61
Red River Delta, 5, 9–10, 20, 26, 37–38, 54
Reeducation camps, 33
Reforestation, 14, 57
Refugees, 33–34
Religion, 44–46. 49. *See also* Buddhism; Christianity; Confucianism, Protestants; Roman Catholics
Resistance movements, 28–30
Reunification, 31–33
Rice, 5, 9–10, 21, 23, 28, 54–55, 59, 63
Rivers, 10–11. *See also* Mekong River; Red River
Roads and highways, 60–61
Roman Catholics, 17, 25, 30, 45
Rural areas, 37–38
Saigon, 15–17, 24, 26, 33, 39, 41. *See also* Ho Chi Minh City
Second Indochina War. *See* Vietnam War
Singapore, 34, 58–59
South China Sea, 6–8, 10–11, 15, 20–21, 34, 56, 60
South Vietnam, 6, 30–33, 49
Southeast Asia, 5–6, 8, 12, 27, 29, 32, 39–40, 47
Soviet Union, 6–7, 28–29, 31, 33–34, 51–53, 59–60
Spratly Islands, 8
Standard of living, 38, 63
Taiwan, 35, 39
Tan Son Nhut airport, 61
Tay Son, 25–26
Tet, 32, 48–49
Tet offensive, 32
Thailand, 10, 26, 34, 41, 54, 57–59
Thailand, Gulf of, 8
Tonkin, 26–27, 29
Tonkin, Gulf of, 8, 10, 17–18, 31
Topography, 9–10
Tourism, 10, 19, 61–63
Trade, 6–7, 21, 25, 32, 34, 58–59, 61
Trade embargo, 32–35, 53, 61
Tran dynasty, 23, 41, 44
Tran Hung Dao, 23
Transportation, 18, 28, 60–61

Trieu Au, 5
Trinh dynasty, 24–25
Trung Nhi, 22
Trung Trac, 22
Truong Son Mountains, 10
Unemployment, 7, 53
United Nations, 34
United States, 6–7, 16, 19, 29, 31–35, 39, 53–54, 61–63
Viet Cong. *See* National Liberation Front
Viet Minh, 6, 29–30
Vietnam
boundaries, size, and location of, 8
divided, 29–32
flag of, 36
population of, 5, 37
reunified, 32–36
Vietnam Airlines, 61
Vietnam, Democratic Republic of. *See* North Vietnam
Vietnam, Republic of. *See* South Vietnam
Vietnam, Socialist Republic of, 32
Vietnam War, 6, 14, 16, 18–19, 31–32, 49, 52, 56, 62
Vietnamese Communist party, 33
Vo Van Kiet, 34
World War 11, 6, 18, 29